Moving on Isn't Easy

M. SOSA

First Printing, 2019

ISBN: 978-1-9992579-0-3

Chapters

Introduction

I know. I know. You've read tons of books and blogs about moving on and they all sound the same. They make you feel worse or make you feel as if you're all alone. I get it.

It won't be easy to get over your ex and definitely won't be easy move on. But, no matter what anybody tells you, only you can make the decision to want better for yourself. I won't try to put a band-aid on your wound because it'll still bleed. I'd rather tell you about my experience and things I did to get over my ex in hope that you'll find comfort in knowing you're not alone.

I'm not a therapist, nor do I pretend to be, but I am a friend, and I believe that reading about parts of my past will guide you towards the right direction.

Moving on is a process. It's not a destination so patience is required because it won't happen overnight.

CHAPTER 1

The Honeymoon Phase

"You're missing someone who's toxic and only brings you heartache. They drain every ounce of your happiness whenever they're around you. They toy with your emotions because they know they'll get away with it. So, no matter how much you feel the need to speak to them, don't. You're worth so much more."

- M. Sosa

I've written paragraphs and deleted them. Written some more and deleted them again. I guess starting this book wasn't as easy as I thought it would be because I knew a lot of emotions and frustrations would flow through these pages. Before I dig in, let me give you a little background about the man I thought was the love of my life. Some of you will see yourself in this situation.

When I was younger, I dated a few men that never matched what I was looking for. I would settle for men that didn't reciprocate the same feelings I did. They were either filled with drama or played head games which was a total turn-off for me.

The more I searched, the more I failed at finding what I longed for until one Valentine's day, I saw him. I was with my girlfriends at an exclusive party that catered to a variety of eligible men and women. There were tons of good-looking men roaming from one side of the room to the next. The problem with me was that whenever I went out to party, it was never to meet a man. I wasn't the type of woman that ever wanted to meet a man while dancing or having drinks. I didn't mind a few dances here and there but anything else would make me feel uncomfortable because I felt I was giving the impression that it would lead to a booty call. That just wasn't my thing.

Throughout the night, I danced with my girlfriend while downing some Jack Daniels. As we were leaving the party, our eyes locked from across the room. Standing in front of me was Adam. For the sake of keeping his real name private that's how I'll refer to my ex.

He was tall, handsome and everything I desired in a man. His eyes gazed straight at me as if we were both stuck in time. It was if we were soulmates that had just seen each other for the first time. Until this day, I can't describe the exuberating feeling I felt because sometimes, when I think about that moment, I still feel those butterflies in my stomach.

The thing about Adam was that we worked at the same place but in different departments. So, we never spoke much to one another except the little "hello's" in the cafeteria. So, that night was different. It felt as though we were meant to meet.

As I approached him, he smiled and started telling me how nice it was to see me there. We spoke for a couple of minutes until my girlfriends rushed me out of the party because they were about to close the doors. As I said goodbye to Adam, I couldn't help but wonder if he was feeling the same things I was feeling.

When I got to my girlfriend's car, I kept telling her how I should've asked Adam for his number. She kept telling me to message him on Monday when I got to work instead.

But that night, I felt persistent in trying to find his number, probably because I had too much to drink. I spent a few hours looking through social media and through mutual friends to see if anybody was up and if anybody would have his number. For the first time ever, I felt as though I had to find Adam's number no matter the cost. It wasn't because I wanted a one-night stand. It was simply because I felt the need to speak to him and see if he was feeling the same way I was. Unfortunately, luck just wasn't on my side that night.

I ended up sending him an email at work on Monday morning, asking him if he had enjoyed the party. When he replied, my heart skipped a beat. We ended up going back and forth, chatting about how fun the party was and what we enjoyed doing on the weekends. After a few days of exchanges, he invited me out. We went on a few dates and eventually ended up at his place. The first night together was heavenly. We couldn't believe we were in each other's arms, kissing and making love to one another. Yeah, I know. You're probably thinking it wasn't lovemaking because it was too soon but the passion we shared was undeniable. It felt like love every time he and I touched.

Adam and I grew close, too fast. His laugh and compassion won me over. I was spending most of my nights at his place but that would eventually be my downfall.

See the thing about meeting someone, getting close to them and spending too much time together too fast will somehow kill the "honeymoon phase." That's exactly what happened between Adam and me.

A few months down the line, he felt as though I was smothering him. I was in his space and he didn't have room for himself. Back in those days, I didn't realize that men wanted to spend time with themselves and not with their girlfriends every two seconds. It's not that they didn't love them. They simply wanted some time apart to hang with the boys or by themselves.

I didn't understand that then, so I kept pushing myself into his plans without getting invited. Even though I knew it was a bit intrusive, I kept at it because I thought it was a way for me to control our relationship. It was also a way for me to know where he was and to make sure he wasn't cheating on me.

Those were my insecurities plaguing my mind because of my past relationships. So many trust issues had me second-guessing my relationship with Adam. Unfortunately, he had to feel the pain for things he hadn't done.

This brought a lot of problems in our relationship especially when he ended it abruptly. One evening, when we had plans to see each other, he called me, but I missed his call. So, I immediately called him back within a couple of minutes but there was no answer. So, I called again… and again… and again… and again.

Even though I originally wanted to reach him because we had plans, I was even more worried that something had happened to him and maybe that's why he wasn't answering the phone. Did he get into a driving accident? Was he mugged? Did someone steal his phone?

I even thought at one point that maybe he was laying in a ditch somewhere because someone had attacked him. I called him almost 20 times within a time span of 5 hours and to no avail, no answer.

I spent days not knowing what was going on until I saw him at work a few days later. As I approached him, what do you think he did? He walked away as if I didn't exist. No remorse. No answers. Only questions tormented my mind. I couldn't understand what I had done.

I found out through his best friend that Adam needed space to think and that he felt offended that I had contacted him so many times. He felt I harassed him and that I could've waited for him to call me back instead of calling non-stop. WHAT? Seriously?

He was upset over pettiness while I was worried that something had happened to him. That made no sense.

At this point, I felt unhinged. A part of me wanted to scream, another part wanted to bash his head in while the other side wanted to feel him in my arms again. Our honeymoon phase ended abruptly, and I was ashamed of having given him all my power. Everything we had worked so hard to build was destroyed over stupidness. That's when I started questioning if all along, he wanted to get out of the relationship but just didn't know how to do it and me calling him a bunch of times was his excuse to end it.

Either way, I knew I wouldn't get an answer, so I had to deal with my heartbreak on my own. That also meant moving on which wasn't as easy as I thought it would be.

CHAPTER 2

Overwhelmed with Confusion and Sadness

"You have to choose yourself even when he doesn't. It won't be easy, but you'll show yourself the respect you deserve."

- M. Sosa

Relationships are all around us. From work relationships to personal relationships, we rely on these relationships to succeed and survive. Because of this, we base a lot of emotions on the people we allow to get close to us. It gives us a sense of meaning. Therefore, when you lose a relationship, you feel disoriented and you're unsure how to proceed. Losing meaning is like losing a part of yourself and not knowing where to go from there.

There's several emotions that run through your mind when a breakup occurs. Confusion and sadness play major roles in it but understanding them will help you reach another level towards moving on.

Confusion

Confusion is a huge part of a heartbreak. We tend to sometimes ignore it because we believe only sadness is supposed to be part of the process but if we learn to differentiate the two, it gets easier to move on.

Did he mean to break it off? Did he mean what he said? Maybe he didn't want to break up? Maybe he still loves me, and he's still confused? A thousand scenarios pop into your head when someone ends a relationship briefly. Those scenarios create a fantasy world that can sometimes overpower your reality.

There were clear signs that he "loved" you, such as the way he treated you and things he said and even the way he said them. If he did all those things, it must've been love, right? I mean, who treats someone so lovingly and shows that they care if they don't want to be with that person, right? Those are all clear signs of confusion.

You'll start overthinking every situation and you'll go over every experience you've been through together wondering where it all went wrong. You'll go through different possibilities but no clear answer to why things happened the way they did. And part of you feels as though the only person that can give you a definite answer is the one that broke your heart.

Sometimes, the reality is staring you right in the face. He just wasn't into you as much as you thought he was. Maybe, he was an asshole and you covered it up because you thought you could change him or maybe he was leading you on to boost his ego. A thousand maybes will go through your head and you know what? You won't get an answer to unravel your confusion so take a step back and accept that things didn't work out. Someday, you'll understand why things didn't work out the way you expected them to.

Sadness

Nobody will fully understand the pain you're going through because we all grieve differently. Even though we all have similar traits, what affected us with one person is different than another.

The one thing that I clearly remember about my breakup with Adam was the feeling of losing full control of my body. I felt my heart break, and I mean it when I say, I felt my heart literally break into a thousand pieces. The person that I trusted with all my heart and soul was the same one shattering it.

I couldn't believe that the same man that said he would protect me and wouldn't cause me the same pain as my previous exes did, was the same one thrusting his knife into me. It was as though something sharp was being driven right through my chest and nothing could stop it.
Adam was right when he said he wouldn't make me go through the same heartbreak again, because what he did was way worse. It wasn't only emotional. It was physical pain I was experiencing. A rush going through my body.

The strong and brave woman I was had been lowered and kicked like a pebble on the side of the street. I felt insignificant. Part of me felt numb while the other part felt every emotion possible screaming through my bones.

How could he put me through this after promising that he wouldn't? I felt pity for myself for the first time in my life.

I wanted to be strong and fearless. I wanted to stand tall and not give a shit about what he had done to me. I wanted to feel like myself again, but I knew this wasn't going to happen anytime soon. I had to feel this heartbreak and had to feel it fully.

Sadness is a common feeling and no matter what you're going through, I can assure you that you're not alone. It's important that you understand that it's normal to feel tons of emotions rushing through you and it's also normal to feel as if you want to cry.

If you need to cry, do it. You'll feel so much better once you let it all out. That doesn't mean that you won't burst into tears at random moments or places because chances are, you will. And it's okay. Nobody expects you to feel 100% and neither should you. But it's also important that you let that sadness out because the longer you hold onto it, the longer it'll take you to heal.

CHAPTER 3

Living in the past

"Never give them the opportunity to disappoint you again."

- M. Sosa

When a relationship ends, we automatically feel a sense of relief when we go back into the past and remember all the good times we shared with that person. We live in the past in fear of accepting what's going on in the present.

Living in the past can make you lose sight of reality. It can also make you create a fictional universe in your head of how you still expect things to be instead of realizing what's happening in real life. Doing this will destroy your ability to enjoy the present moment. Here are a few tricks on how to stop living in the past:

Examine your life now and how the past affected your present

It's important to know where you're coming from and where you're headed. Many people fail to do this on the regular because let's face it; life gets in the way. And sometimes our priorities aren't about understanding our past, present and future because we're too busy with work, with family, with life.

But in order to let go of your past, you must acknowledge all the situations that made you cry and smile because they helped you shape you into the beautiful human being you are today.

Sometimes, you have no choice but to take a step

back and reevaluate how the past has affected your present. Unfortunately, that also means reminiscing about hurtful events that may trigger something in you but it's equally important to remember the good times that made you smile. You shouldn't erase everything when certain moments had a positive impact in your life.

Reminiscing about all these events is a way for you to understand what happened then and to also make the effort to *leave the past in the past*. Once you've acknowledged everything that happened to you that made you into the person you are today, you'll be able to focus on living in the present.

You can't fully examine your life if you're still living in denial either. You need to realize that everything happened for a reason and the only way you're going to get over the past is by making peace with it.

Accept that every experience that's happened so far in your life was for a reason. It may have not been blue skies and rainbows but you're here now and growing from those experiences is a step towards the right direction.

Explore your past feelings

There are many things that can trigger locked up

hurtful feelings so it's important to never ignore your past. Many people tend to pretend they don't matter when in reality, those feelings are holding their lives hostage.

While it's never easy to go back and explore why and what is hurting you, it's a way to cope with those emotions and expressing them in whatever way is most comfortable to you.

You can easily speak to a friend, family or even a therapist. Anybody that you know will listen and won't judge you but will guide you towards the right way of handling things is the right person to speak to.

You can also write down your feelings in a secret journal that nobody else needs to read but you, or you can write a letter to the person that caused you pain without mailing it out. Sometimes writing things is a lot easier than expressing them to people around you.

I've done this many times and I've always sensed peace after spilling my emotions on paper.

Whichever way you choose, remember that your main focus is to let all those emotions go.

Now keep in mind that sometimes there are good

memories that affect your life. When you dwell on the "good times" you shared with someone, they can lead you to long for moments that no longer exist and that will stop you from focusing on your present life.

Focus on the things you can change

I know how it feels like to want to change things or certain situations from your past. But let's face it, we all have a colored past and some of us have it worse than others. Unfortunately, there's no time machine to take you back into the past and make those changes. There are things that you simply have to learn to live with, no matter how it makes you feel.

There are experiences in your life that you may never fully understand or know why they occurred but that doesn't mean you can hold onto the important lessons they taught you.

In order to make peace with your past, you need to realize that you're wasting valuable energy on things that you cannot change. There are things in life that unfortunately can't be undone. Even though you can't undo the past, you can modify the way you handle and understand it.

Your energy is valuable so keep that in mind

whenever certain thoughts pop into your head.

Focus on the present

This is a tough one because it's not easy to let go of once happened to you especially if you're still holding on to those emotions. But once you're honest and willing to let go, you will. You can't undo past mistakes, but you can make the best of your life.

Living your life in the now means exactly that. Live every moment as if it were your last. Enjoy your day-to-day, no matter what it is. Focus on being present here and now. When you start telling your subconscious that you're focusing on what's happening in the present, you automatically think less about the past. Don't get me wrong, there'll probably be moments when some of those past memories creep up on you but it's crucial that you acknowledge them for a brief moment and then let them fade in the back of your mind.

It's healthy to give yourself pep talks, too. Repeat to yourself that everything you've been through was part of your past and you're creating your own happiness in the present. Keeping a positive outlook like this will avoid you digging in too deep in your mind.

Remember, the point is to avoid reminiscing on the hurt and pain. So, it's important to ignore all the negative memories and focus solely on how things are going to get better.

This also means that life will throw different challenges your way and you'll have to face them head on, just as you did in the past. They're going to test you to make sure you're learning from your old mistakes and that you're willing to make the necessary changes to let go of the past and to make way for the future. So, take chances and live your best life.

CHAPTER 4
Let Go of the Fantasy

"Stop hurting yourself by going back to the person that hurt you. Even if you think they're going to change, they won't. They'll never be right for you."

- M. Sosa

This chapter hurts and some of you may get offended by what I'm about to say because deep within you know it's the truth.

Real love is not based on fantasy. One of the first steps to moving forward is getting over the denial phase. Often, people forget that the relationship ended and tend to obsess over someone that isn't reciprocating the same feelings they are.

The problem is when you project your dreams and hopes while hoping that the other person will make them a reality. But when they don't, you still persist because you believe that they're meant to love you. The hope that someday they'll feel the same way is what keeps you stuck for months or maybe even years. Ask yourself one question. Are they reciprocating the same love right back at you? The answer is most likely no.

It may feel as though your ex wants to still be with you when they keep messaging or calling you or might still be sleeping with you, so it gives you the impression they still want a "relationship" with you. That's not always the case. Sometimes, exes just want to keep in touch and remain cordial, or simply want sex because it comforts them. That doesn't mean they want a committed relationship again.

This is why it's so important to speak to one another about what's going on because if you don't, you might end up creating a fantasy of what you hope things will be like.

Running after this person becomes like a gambling addiction because it feeds your obsession. You keep playing frequently in hopes that someday, you'll win the big prize (him). Maybe this time, when you play the machine, you'll finally win (his heart). By doing so, you take the chance of becoming infatuated with the desire of wanting to be with them even if they're not showing you the same feelings in return. It's as if you're hoping that maybe the next time you feed the machine more money, maybe you'll win, and he'll want to be with you. But that's far from the truth because all you're doing is waiting for the big payoff by putting in coin after coin after coin and getting no reward. And you keep wishing that maybe the next coin will be the big winner but that never happens.

This happened with Adam, time and time again because I allowed him to do whatever he wanted with me. He knew he had me in the palm of his hands because I'd do anything to get his attention. I would drop whatever I was doing to be by his side and would make sure he had everything he needed from food to money to sex. I was so excited each time he called that it didn't matter that he dismissed me after I had dropped everything for him. It was the fact that he had chosen ME and not someone else. I was honored that out of all the women he could've picked, it was me he chose and that kept me coming back for more.

He kept me hoping that if I tried harder or gave him more, maybe next time would be my lucky day and I would finally win the big reward. I mean, at the end of the day, I had invested so much of my time, money and affection; how could he not choose me, right? Wrong. He knew I was addicted to him, but he did nothing to spare my heart. It was an empty game.

He didn't want me. I couldn't see it because I was too infatuated with wanting him for myself again. I didn't want to lose what we once had. I wanted to be the only one in his eyes. The one that did everything for him.

That's the issue with people that become obsessed with their exes. They create a world of fantasy where they imagine how life can be with this person and no matter how much they get hurt; they don't realize it because they're too focused on winning the prize instead of realizing that they're hurting themselves in the process.

It's an intoxicating feeling that takes over your

body because you know you deserve better, but you're so consumed with wanting to be with this person that it clouds your judgement.

People that suffer from a romantic obsession need to realize that these types of "relationships" never work out, no matter how much you try. It's an empty gamble that will only shatter your heart. When someone isn't reciprocating the same feelings you are, this is your cue to leave. No, you shouldn't try harder. No, you shouldn't keep playing silly head games in hope that he'll change his mind. You're not going to win his heart because if he wanted to be with you; he would be with you already.

When the relationship isn't reciprocal and he sporadically tries to reconnect with you; no matter how hard you persist and try to win his heart, you won't. Eventually, you'll end up emotionally drained and broken over something you could've avoided from the get-go.

Obsession isn't an easy pattern to break. You want to fix him and believe you're the only one that can help him. No matter how unpleasant he acts with you, you persist in trying to heal him because you can't help but understand what he's feeling. You want to rescue him. You want to be his savior because you hope that eventually, he'll be able to rescue you. What you're not realizing is that your obsession is taking over your reality and what you're imagining as yourself as a couple is nothing more than a mere friendship or booty call.

The fact that you're unsure of his feelings makes you want him more. You can't help but want to help him because you believe that if you stick by his side and become his ride or die, that he'll eventually love you the way you love him. You fantasize that he'll eventually open his eyes and he'll see everything you've done for him.

You're creating a movie inside your head... a fairytale of how you wish things will turn out. Kind of like those Disney movies where the Princess ends up with the Prince at the end. He kisses her and they end up living happily ever after.

One of the main reasons why you can't move on is because you keep imagining him as the "right man" for you. You can't see yourself with anyone else but him. Those type of fixations aren't healthy because they can lead you to fixate on the wrong things such as believing you will eventually be together once the circumstances change or when the timing is right. All of these are signs that he isn't the right one for you.

Think about it, if it was meant to be, you would be

together now, no matter what.

It's never easy to admit to yourself that you have a problem because you become consumed by the obsession. You believe it isn't a one-sided fantasy. You believe everything you're experiencing with this person is for real and that they also love you, they just don't know it yet. Doesn't that sound a little crazy?

You're so sure that someday, they will fall head over heels for you and that somewhere down the line, they'll realize you were always "the one."

Now, how do you get over this obsession? There's no easy way out of it until you start accepting that things are only a mere figment of your imagination. It'll be heartbreaking and it'll take time until you're mature enough to realize that things will never be the way you want them to be.

It's a process so don't try to rush it. It won't happen overnight, nor will it happen in a week. It might actually take years but once you're in the right state of mind, you'll find it a lot easier to see things with a clearer mind.

No matter how much someone tells you to stop caring or to stop being emotionally available for that person, chances are you won't be able to because you'll still feel compelled to stay available whenever he calls. This is what you need to break away from or it'll keep haunting you.

You'll begin to break free from this obsession when you decide to stop calling him or you stop him from coming over late for those meaningless booty calls. Keeping in constant contact with him isn't going to help your situation. It'll just make it tougher to let go.

Those tasks might not be as easy as you think but when you're willing to change your behavior, you'll start seeing change within yourself. You may not be able to change your feelings, but you can make the effort to modify your behavior towards him.

When you realize that you're stopping yourself from having meaningful relationships with people who actually want to be with you, you'll make the effort to change.

Eventually, you'll realize that this toxic behavior is distracting you from your own pain which is also stopping your personal growth. That might be what triggers you to want better for yourself. Even though your ex fills a big space in your heart and mind, you'll eventually realize that he doesn't define you and that'll be your breaking point. That'll be the moment you finally exhale.

Once you start to break free, you'll feel different because you'll no longer feel imprisoned by thoughts of him. You'll be more rational, and you might even realize how degrading you've been to yourself throughout the years.

You'll no longer feel consumed by him because you'll feel free. You'll realize that you weren't only mourning the loss of your ex but also the loss of the fantasy, and that's the key in how to move on.

CHAPTER 5

Reinvent Yourself

"You have a heart of gold. You're willing to sacrifice everything to make others happy without asking for anything in return. Even the ones that hurt you don't deserve your kindness but you're willing to always help others no matter what they've done to you. That's what makes you one of a kind."

- M. Sosa

After a breakup, most people lose themselves because they're continuously thinking about what they could've done or said to make things work. Because of this, they tend to forget about themselves and their needs.

In order to move on, I found it easier when I reinvented myself. I felt the need to let go of the old and bring in the new. Here are a few ways that may guide you towards a new you:

Change your hair

This is my favorite one because it's so empowering to make a drastic change with your hair. Whether you chop it, dye it or style it differently, you'll feel like a Queen sitting on a throne. It'll boost your self-esteem and it'll also make you feel brand new.

Sometimes, changing your hair color from a brunette to a blonde can make a huge difference on the way you perceive yourself, or maybe cutting your long hair to a short bob can make you feel sexier and more appealing.

No matter what you try, a change in hairstyle might help you change the perception you have of yourself.

Rearrange the rooms in your house

Nothing is tougher than staying somewhere you shared with your ex. Sometimes, just switching the furniture around can create a new perspective and might also change your mind.

Some people tend to throw away or sell their old furniture because they'd rather buy new ones to avoid thinking about their ex. I've had friends purchase new beds because the thought of sleeping in the bed their ex was in would cause them anxiety. So, if you have the money to switch it all up, go for it. Redecorate and rearrange, maybe a new Zen looking place isn't so bad after all.

Buy new clothes

I've noticed throughout the years that buying new clothes is therapy to overcoming a breakup.

Maybe the clothes you used to wear are old fashioned or outdated. Changing them might heighten your personality but they will help you gain confidence. It will rejuvenate the way you perceive yourself.

Stop listening to old songs

One of the things we tend to do when going

through a breakup is listening to the same old sappy songs that remind us of our exes. While there's nothing wrong with doing so, it can be counterproductive when you're trying so hard to forget them.

I did this way too many times with music I used to listen to with Adam. There was a particular song he dedicated to me from J. Holiday called "It's Yours" that always put a smile on my face. And every time I heard that song play after our breakup, tears would come rolling down my face. It was hurtful to hear a song that used to bring me so much joy become a painful memory. To be quite honest, whenever I hear that song play now, I change songs because I don't want to remember anything about those times. Sometimes, it's best to leave certain things in the past and for me, it's that song.

Listening to old love songs that remind you of specific moments with your ex are going to hurt you more than heal you. So, there's nothing wrong with exploring new artists or a new genre of music.

Maybe even going to a concert from an artist you normally wouldn't listen to might help you change your perspective. There's nothing wrong in trying new music.

Find new hobbies

While you may already have a few hobbies you're working on, it doesn't mean you can't add a few more to your list.

When Adam and I broke up, a huge part of me wanted to get over the overthinking and the sleepless nights so I joined the gym. It was one of the best things I ever did because it kept my mind at ease but also helped me reflect more on myself. I felt the need to do something new.

The gym might not be for everyone but that doesn't mean that some other form of activity won't pique your interest. There are classes of pottery, painting, martial arts, and so much more to choose from.

Reexamine your life and what you want

When reinventing yourself, you'll want to think about the things you really want versus the things you don't.

Learning from the lessons you've been given will guide you towards happier moments in your life. So, take the necessary time to focus on the things that didn't work out and also the things that will work out the next time.

When you reexamine your life, you look at it from a different perspective so you can live your best life without the hassle.

All I'm trying to tell you is that you shouldn't be pouting all the time in a corner with a bucket of ice cream by your side. Pick yourself up and make yourself feel like a million dollars. Sometimes, it's as easy as putting on some makeup, dressing up and going out. Live a little instead of staying miserable at home reminiscing about things you cannot change.

I've noticed the more I smiled after a breakup, the happier I became and the less I thought about my ex. Try it even though it might feel forced at first, eventually you'll find yourself smiling for real and for good reasons.

CHAPTER 6

It's Okay to Still to Still Love Them

"I still love you. I probably always will but that doesn't mean I have to hold on to the idea that we'll be together again someday. I deserve to move on even if it's without you."

- M. Sosa

It's not easy to stop loving someone especially when you've shared some of the most intimate moments with them. Many people love their exes for some period of time after a breakup because the emotions and wounds are still fresh.

Unfortunately, some stay stuck in love for years because they believe nobody else will ever fill that void. They're afraid of meeting someone new because they fear getting hurt again.

But I'll be the first to tell you that there's nothing wrong with still loving your ex. It's normal to still have feelings. Just because someone breaks up with you doesn't mean that the feeling of love stops.

Moving on from a relationship that ended isn't always about ending the love you feel inside. A part of you may feel torn while another side of you knows that the best thing you can do is move on with your life. Sometimes, the only way to move on is by wishing your ex the best and want what's best for them even when that means not being together.

I know it's not easy to wish them well especially when they caused you pain and broke your heart into a thousand pieces. There's a part of you that wants to see them suffer while another part of you wants things to go back to the way they used to be. I get it. I've been there, too.

Feelings don't stop when someone walks out of your life. Those feelings linger and sometimes, they stay longer than we expect them to because we're not ready to let go. It's normal. So, don't assume you're supposed to automatically flush them out of your system.

People change. Feelings change. Seasons change but your love for your ex might still be present because you're in love with the memories and all the joy they once brought you. You can't forget those moments, but you can bury them deep within your mind so they're not constantly the first thing you think about.

Your love has the capacity to evolve and change over time. It's a process that encompasses caring for a person who you spent a long period of time with but removing the romantic side from it. The moment you remove that romantic aspect from the "love" you feel for the person, you'll facilitate your healing process because your emotional side won't be as affected as it used to be.

The real question most people ask is how long is it reasonable to still have feelings for your ex? There's no accurate answer for this because it varies depending on the person and the history you shared.

I've said this in my previous books because it rings so much truth. What may take someone days or weeks to get over a breakup and the emotions attached to it, it may take someone else months or years to move on from an ex. After spending so much time with this person, it's normal to feel an ongoing attachment that's harder to shake off. We all heal and love differently, so you can't expect someone to get over what they're feeling because it was easier for you to do it. You must let them heal at their own pace.

When you go through a breakup, you're not only losing the person you loved. You're also losing his side of the family, that you probably met, the plans you both made for the future and maybe even your intentions to start a family. Nothing will make sense for a while because you're adapting to

being alone again, and you're trying to understand where everything went wrong or why things didn't work out.

But, the months that follow a breakup are the perfect time to practice self-love. It's never easy to accept the situation for what it is so it's important to keep an eye out on your mental well-being.

Sometimes, your emotions can lead to depression or anxiety because those never fading emotions keep lingering on. If you let those emotions take over, you risk the chance of falling down a hole so deep that might take you longer to get out from. The best thing to do if you feel you're falling into a depression is to seek help.

It's always helpful to speak to someone else that can guide you in the right direction whether it be a therapist or psychologist. Anybody that can help your grieving process.

Eventually, when you're ready, those loving feelings you have towards your ex will slowly start to fade. You'll notice your life changing and you'll also realize how much you've grown from this experience.

Every time someone mentions his name, you'll reminisce for a few seconds about how you used to feel about him, but you'll know have the right tools to help you move past it.

CHAPTER 7

There's Nothing Wrong with You

"You did everything right. You tried to put things back in place when they were falling apart. You moved mountains to repair whatever was broken in your relationship even though it didn't work out. Even though he didn't realize everything you did; you should be proud of yourself because you tried. That's the most important part."

- M. Sosa

Let's start this chapter off on a positive note. YOU ARE ENOUGH. There's nothing wrong with you.

There is no such thing as perfection. Even your favorite celebrities have pimples, bad skin, rolls, and the list goes on. Even somebody obsessed with self-improvement will eventually see they're not perfect.

The problem most of us have after a breakup is that we believe when someone leaves us that we're not good enough. That's far from the truth. Just because you didn't embody what your ex was looking for doesn't mean there's something wrong with you. It simply means you weren't the right match. Period. Nothing else.

You're your own punching bag at this point because you keep putting negative thoughts in your mind about yourself. You're human and you should always remember that. There's nothing wrong with you. You're more than enough and the right person will know it.

Here's a little list that proves you're fine:

You make mistakes like everybody else

You're going to make mistakes. It's part of human nature. Those mistakes allow you to learn as you go. You get to reflect on them, take it in and try to better the next time around. Lighten up. You're doing the best that you can.

You're unique

It doesn't matter if you're extroverted, outgoing, creative, etc. All that matters is that you realize that you're unique and there's nobody else like you.

You're doing the best that you can

Life isn't meant to have all the right answers. It's a learning process and you're doing the best that you can. Sometimes, you're too hard on yourself instead of taking a step back and realizing that you're doing a great job by surviving.

You feel and that's a good thing

You feel. You hurt. You bleed. You respond to all of these and that's good news. Some people don't feel anything or have no remorse for anything they do but the fact that you do is a great thing.

You don't deserve to get hurt

Nobody deserves to get their heart broken. Nobody. All of this to say, you're more than enough and if someone doesn't realize how wonderful you are. That's their problem, not yours.

So, even though you feel the need to blame yourself for the breakup—DON'T! You did all that you could and sometimes life has a way of throwing curveballs your way but that doesn't mean you have to keep lowering your self-esteem because you feel that you weren't good enough.

Shit happens. Life happens. You are worth so much more than you give yourself credit for and the more you start giving yourself these pep talks, the more you'll start feeling about yourself and the entire situation.

CHAPTER 8

Realizing he Wasn't the Right One for You

"The toughest thing I had to face was
knowing you weren't the right one for me
but still believing I could change you."

- M. Sosa

This is going to be your toughest job because realizing and accepting that he wasn't the right one for you will most likely break you at first.

When someone is serious about you, they make every effort possible to show you. They don't let things drag along for years because they're unsure what they really want. I'm not saying people automatically know they want a serious relationship from the get-go because sometimes, love flourishes at the oddest moment.

But if they wanted to make you their wife or girlfriend, they would have. It took me a long while to accept this but once I did, I saw things more clearly.

It was tough to accept the fact that Adam didn't want to be with me anymore. I had given him my all and in return, all he gave me was heartbreak. I was so consumed by my addiction to him that I didn't want to accept that he wasn't the right one for me. I believed from the bottom of my heart that we were meant to be.

I saw him as my soulmate, as the man I wanted to marry. But yet, I couldn't see that he didn't see or feel the same way. All he wanted was friendship at this point, nothing more. I had a hard time believing it because I felt it in my gut that he was the one I was supposed to end up with. Nobody else would ever do.

I couldn't imagine myself with someone else and I think that's why, throughout the years, any man I dated wasn't enough. They weren't like Adam. They were either too short, too tall, too skinny, too fat, too different. No matter who I dated, I would always compare them to Adam.

It wasn't a competition but in the back of my mind, I made it into one. I expected someone to measure up against him and because of this I ended up pushing good men away. If someone would simply come close to being similar to Adam, maybe I'd take a leap of faith and try to move on. But nobody ever did.

Eventually, I realized that he wasn't my soulmate because if he was, I wouldn't be trying to find his "twin" because the real Adam would be with me. No matter how I tried to spin it, there was no way he was the right one for me. He proved to me time and time again that he wasn't into me anymore.

Our time had passed and as tough as it was to admit it to myself, I had to face reality if I wanted to move forward with my life. I couldn't keep comparing everybody to him and I definitely couldn't keep looking for him in the people that wanted to be a part of my life. If I wanted to move on, I had to admit that he wasn't who I wanted him to be and that was okay.

You're going to end up fighting with yourself because a part of you will believe he was the right one for you and you should try to make things work, even if it's not what he wants. Another part of you will know that he isn't the right one for you but will try to make you see the truth that's in front of you.

Facing reality will be one of the toughest things you'll go through after a breakup but it's also one of the most liberating feelings because you come to terms with everything that's been going on. And sometimes, admitting to yourself that the person you fell in love with wasn't the right one for you can help you heal and can help push you towards moving on.

CHAPTER 9

Avoid Contacting Him

"It's the memories that make me want to
keep running back to you even though
I know it'll only end up hurting me.
I have to learn to let you go."

- M. Sosa

If you want to get over your breakup, you need to reduce contact with the person that broke you. I know it won't be easy. It'll take a lot of adjustments but during your healing period, you're more fragile and need to focus on bettering yourself.

You don't need a constant reminder of the person that tore your heart into pieces but when you contact or see them, you're rubbing more salt on your wound. Why keep doing that to yourself? Your heart deserves some tender love and care. Which means keeping it away from anyone or anything that might cause it more harm. Let your heart rest.

No matter how your relationship ended, you need time to process what happened. You also need time to reflect on how to make yourself whole again. It won't happen quickly no matter how much you wish for it, but as long as you steer away from the person that hurt you, you have a better chance at healing faster.

If you have to block them from social media accounts to avoid seeing how they're living, do it. If you have to block them from calling or texting you to feel some peace of mind, do it. Do whatever you have to do to make yourself feel better.

This also means you shouldn't be breaking up on a Saturday and start hanging out on Sunday. That's pointless and you're only going to end up causing yourself more pain. I'm not saying you shouldn't be friends with that person because we all have different terminologies to what a "friendship" is but you should give it time and space to let things simmer down. Eventually, if you're both capable of keeping that friendship alive without feeling a sense of remorse, go right ahead.

Adam and I decided to stay friends a few years down the line. We started off hanging out as friends but eventually started sleeping with one another again. There wasn't supposed to be any emotional attachment but unfortunately, feelings got in the way. We couldn't differentiate what a "friendship" and a "f*ck friend" were. This caused a lot of tension between us and we ended up parting ways several times throughout the years. I remember regretting letting him back in every single time he left me. The dunce cap had to come off if I wanted to move on with my life.

Avoid contacting the person that hurt you. You'll probably start writing a text that has several paragraphs and you'll debate on sending it because you're unsure if they'll reply. You know that gut feeling you get at moments like that? That's a sign you shouldn't be sending it. Whatever you do, don't hit that "send" button. You'll thank me later. You need to give yourself enough time and space to start the healing process and you can't heal if that person is constantly in your face or your thoughts.

There's also nothing wrong if you hate them and never want to see them again. That's a plus for you but once again, keep your distance. Sometimes, when we're mad at someone that caused the breakup, we tend to want to see them pay for their actions so we're constantly seeking information about them. That's a big NO NO. Let shit go.

It's going to probably hurt you when you stop speaking to them and a ton of memories will come flashing back but if you're looking for a way to move forward, you have to make the right decision of staying away from them.

Some people move from their hometown in order to avoid contact with their ex and I can't blame them. Not everybody has the ability to move so easily but if it's going to give you peace of mind, pack up those bags and start somewhere new.

At the end of the day, you're trying to heal and avoiding any type of encounter will help you towards the right path.

CHAPTER 10

Being Single is Great

"You're not broken, sweetheart.
You're just adapting to being alone
again and finding the strength within to
love yourself unconditionally. You'll
overcome all the pain you're going
through... patience."

- M. Sosa

Stop glorifying relationships. There's nothing wrong with being single. Whether you're in a relationship or not, there'll still be challenges and lessons.

When I was with Adam, I loved the companionship. I enjoyed the time we spent going out to movies, restaurants, dates but there was also a part of me that got stuck believing that being in a relationship was better than being single. I thought that if I didn't have him in my life, my life wouldn't mean a thing. I was wrong. Even if you're single, it doesn't add more value to your life by being with someone.

Being single can seem scary at first because you don't know what to expect but you shouldn't be afraid of it. It's a perfect opportunity for growth and to get to know yourself better.

There's beauty in being single. You can do whatever you've always wanted to do without having to think about your partner's feelings or having them tag along.

Things that you always dreamed of doing are things you should be putting on your bucket list. It's time to improve anything that you feel that isn't as it should be.

Nowadays, there's a constant rush for people

to get married or to be in a committed relationship when the best relationship you'll ever have is with yourself. You don't need anyone to be happy. Remember that.

Many singles are just as happy as those who are paired up. I believe that's because most people feel relieved they don't have to go through all the ups and downs that couples sometimes go through.

One of the toughest things is coping with the breakup and feeling as if you have to start all over again, alone. Even getting back into the dating game is tough because you don't remember how to act single.

There are many benefits to being single and embracing them will help your growth process.

Being single allows you to become more focused on things you may have let slide or haven't taken into consideration. Some people focus on their career because it gives them a goal to achieve while others focus on their health because they know that having more energy will keep them motivated. There are others that take this time to put their focus on themselves. It's a great thing if you're doing this because you're showing yourself self-care and that's the best gift you can ever give yourself.

But my favorite thing when I was single was having the independence to do whatever I wanted without having to answer to anybody else. I could go travel, go out and party, relax at home, pick up a hobby, go to the gym... pretty much do anything without having to think about making plans with my partner. It's not that you need anybody's approval either because that would be them controlling you but it's the fact that you're free to do as you please without explanations.

You can simply pick up and go whenever you want. You could always do those things as a couple but knowing you don't need to tell anybody what you're doing gives you a sense of freedom. There's no pressure and you don't have to worry about a second opinion.
This is your time. Enjoy it. Live it fully. Take this time to prepare yourself for your next relationship but whatever you do, don't rush it. Learn about yourself and fix whatever needs fixing.

Don't jump into the next relationship because you're afraid of being single. When people do that, they end up settling for less and sometimes end up staying in unhappy relationships for years because they believe they don't deserve any better. Loneliness is horrible but that doesn't mean you have to jump into another relationship to fill that void.

Some people find discomfort with spending time with themselves. Their desire to be in a relationship clouds their mind because they don't want to "waste" time getting to know who they truly are. They'd rather conform to society's belief that being single is "bad" while being in a relationship means that you're "normal." None of this is true.

It's normal to want companionship, to communicate with others, to share ideas but you have to get it out of your head that being in a relationship automatically means that you'll be happy.

I know many people that are in committed relationships or married, and they're the unhappiest they've ever been. Some of them don't speak with their partners, others constantly cheat while others stay only because there's kids involved. This isn't healthy. I'm not telling you to leave the father of your children, but I am telling you to pay attention to what you're showing them. Children aren't stupid. They can feel when two parents are in a toxic relationship and many times, will mimic the same behavior of their parents when they're grown up.

There's also many singles living their best lives because there's no emotional attachment, no drama, no worrying... no stress. Just living each day as if it's their last. They live happily because they don't need to worry about someone else. They're more worried about their well-being and happiness.

That's why it's important to break free from the thought that being with someone means you'll be happy. Be happy single before you start looking for love.

CHAPTER 11

The
Victim Role

"Yes, they hurt you but that doesn't mean you have to keep playing the victim to get sympathy from others. You're stronger than you think. Show it."

- M. Sosa

Playing the victim has happened to a few of us but the important part is getting out of that phase.

What you're feeling matters and even though many won't understand what you're going through, it doesn't mean you have to play the victim and blame others. I'm not saying your feelings aren't important or you shouldn't be upset at the situations that have happened to you. But I'm telling you that playing the victim isn't healthy and can prevent you from moving forward.

I used to blame Adam for everything that went wrong in my life after our breakup. At the time, I couldn't see clearly because I didn't want to. I believed that everything I was doing was right and he was to blame for anything not going right. He was the wrongdoer. I was the victim.

I refused to admit that I had control over my life and whatever went wrong at this point had nothing to do with him. It all had to do with the way I perceived myself and the things I accepted. I had to take responsibility for my actions and my thoughts. I had to take responsibility to be happy because it wasn't up to him to make me feel that way.

Why do people play the victim?

I'm guilty of this. I used to play the victim because I

wanted people to feel pity for me and wanted people to tend to my needs. This was a huge part of my downfall until I realized that playing the victim was also keeping me stuck in a broken state and if I didn't correct my behavior, I wouldn't move forward with my life.

There are several reasons why people take on the victim mentality and sometimes, they don't realize they're even doing it. Most people that act this way have been a victim of other people's wrongdoings or have suffered some type of misfortune through the hands of someone they trusted.

From the most part, a victim mentality can develop from family situations during childhood. This is why criminals act the way they do. They believe they're in no wrong and that someone with authority is unfairly singling them out. Whatever the reason behind it is, living with a "victim" is hard. It can easily drain your energy and you might even feel exhausted while in their company.

How do you recognize someone with a victim mentality? Here are a few examples of traits they have. You might see yourself in this list, too.

People that play the victim will:

Try to control others

Someone who plays the role of a victim will oftentimes try to control others into believing they're in the wrong, while they're always right. Unfortunately for those that don't know any better, they'll easily fall into the control of a "victim" out of pity or because they believe everything this person is saying.

That doesn't mean the victim is evil or manipulative because sometimes, the victim doesn't even realize what they're doing.

Won't take responsibility for their actions

The victim has trouble facing reality so if something's their fault, they won't accept responsibility for their actions. They prefer to point the finger at someone else in order to avoid being blamed, or they might also ignore their role in creating the problem.

They tend to act as "martyrs" instead of a "victim".

Hold onto grudges

We all know someone that loves to hold on to grudges. They carry them around like weapons in case they feel threatened or feel the need to get out of a situation. Sometimes, they hold onto those grudges to throw them back in your face to try to make you feel bad for them.

A victim will bring up bad memories when the opportunity arises in order to help them gain the upper hand.

They use these memories so they can make changes to their circumstances.
No matter how much you try to convince them to let go of those grudges, they hold onto them like glue. It's a security blanket.

Act like they're perfect and will criticize others

The victim has to feel superior than others in order to feed their ego. They don't necessarily do it on purpose. They have low self-esteem so degrading someone else makes them feel better. Putting others down makes them feel as if they're perfect and others are below them. They'll find faults in anybody around them, even if they don't know them.

Some might have narcissistic tendencies that make them arrogant and this causes them to not trust anybody that comes into their lives. The victim will make assumptions that everybody is untrustworthy like them.

Take advantage of your kindness

Victims will take advantage of your kindness because they want you to feel pity for them. "Look at me. Poor me." They're like vampires, sucking all the energy out of you and once they're done, they'll throw you to the curb.

They'll always manage to get your attention especially in times when you're not focusing on them. Sometimes, the victim will ask you to do things for them that they are fully capable of doing. They simply want someone else to take care of those tasks for them.

How do you stop playing the victim?

Here are a few tips and tricks that helped me along the way. They might be useful to you if you see yourself playing the victim role.

Be compassionate towards yourself

Practice self-love and that means showing yourself each day that you matter and start each morning by telling yourself something positive. It could be as simple as looking yourself in the mirror and telling yourself how beautiful you are even if you don't fully feel it.

Replace self-loathing with self-compassion. Tell yourself each day how wonderful it is to be you. No matter how tough it is to get out of bed or how tough it is to tell yourself something positive, do it. It all starts with one kind thing you say to yourself.

Explore your wounds and why you feel the need to play the victim. Once you start to understand the reason behind it, you'll find it easier to fall back in love with yourself.

Start using statements with "I"

Empower yourself with statements beginning with "I" and you'll notice a shift in your life. When positive energy starts flowing within you, you'll drastically change everything around you.

When you learn to say "I can" or "I will" to situations that are thrown your way, instead of replying with a negative response such as "I can't" or "I won't", there's something within you that changes because you feel you can overcome anything. That's taking self-responsibility for your happiness.

Deciding to take on a new way of thinking, in other words, changing your mindset, can be very beneficial for how you see yourself.

Perform acts of kindness towards others

Playing the victim means you're solely focused on

yourself and what you can get out of it. But when you decide to do something for someone else, there's a joy that comes over your body because you know you did something right even though you didn't have to.

It's a great feeling knowing you don't have to manipulate others to get what you want. And it's an even better feeling knowing you did something to make someone else smile.

This is also a way to stop self-victimization.

Start seeing yourself as a survivor and no longer a victim

When you keep putting in your head that you're a victim, that's all you'll be but when you start seeing yourself as a survivor, you'll start taking back control of your life.

A victim believes they're helpless and that's not who you want to be anymore so take the necessary steps to overcome that feeling.

Once you begin taking the steps towards being a survivor, you'll see life clearer and you'll attract the right people to join you on your journey. All the negativity will start leaving your body because it'll be replenished with all the positive things you believe in.

Be responsible for your decisions

It's never an easy task to be honest with yourself but I noticed throughout the years that the more open and honest I was with myself, the happier I became.

It's not the greatest feeling to gain sympathy from others while still pointing the fingers at others, so why do it? Being responsible for your life and your decisions will help you gain a lot of clarity. You don't want to be known as someone that's a victim. You'd rather be known as someone who overcame hardships, pushed through and survived, right?

You're responsible for your life. Find ways to build your confidence and believe that you're capable of achieving great things. It's equally important to reflect on things that happened in your past and how you overcame them.

Ask yourself why you're suffering

Most of the pain I ever felt was because I attached myself to thoughts that had me overthinking. This made me suffer. In other words, I caused my own suffering and I stayed in that mentality because I didn't want to get out of it. I let those thoughts invade my mind. But once I started acknowledging that these thoughts had no power over me unless I let, things started getting easier.

The easier things got, the easier it became to move on with my life.

Remember, you don't have to let your thoughts take over your life. They'll only take over if you let them which means you are in total control of how you handle them. Try practicing meditation. That helped me realize that our thoughts have no meaning unless we allow them to stay stuck in our heads.

Can anything good come out of being a victim?

I'm thankful for everything that I did back then because I wouldn't be the woman I am today. If you take this experience as something positive, you'll realize how much you've grown from it.

If you hadn't gone through self-victimization, you might have never understood what it means to be responsible for your own happiness and might have never realized how empowering it is to come out of a dark hole.

When you stop playing the victim, you become a completely different person on the inside and the outside because things aren't only about you.

Life isn't easy but you're in charge of the choices you make and that includes feeling good about yourself and feeling bad about another person's actions. Take responsibility for YOUR actions. That means taking control of your happiness and not giving your energy to people who did you wrong. When you do that, you end up giving them power over your well-being when they shouldn't even be part of the equation.

Yes, they hurt you and it sucked but you also have the ability to say "Enough is enough. I'm not giving this person my energy anymore." They hurt you in ways only you know but that doesn't mean you have to keep giving them that energy and attention any longer.

When you keep blaming others, all you're giving yourself is temporary relief over your pain and suffering. It won't be helpful in the long run and you'll end up feeling worse than ever as time goes by. Wouldn't you want to let that negative energy go? Isn't it time to set yourself free from all those problems?

Each time you feel as if you're going to blame someone for whatever reason, ask yourself what your role in the situation is and how you can fix it. Most of the time, you'll notice that you have a choice in how you respond to the situation. Either you let shit go or you hold a grudge that will eat you up inside each time you think about it. Remind yourself that you have the ability to either be hopeful or helpless in any situation that's placed in front of you.

CHAPTER 12

Forgiveness

"She's proof that even when broken,
she's still a fighter."

- M. Sosa

Forgiveness is one of the toughest steps when trying to move on.

It took me years to forgive Adam for my broken heart, the broken promises and for being the complete opposite type of man he said he'd never be. I wallowed in my pain because I felt that the longer I played the victim, that eventually I'd forget him and all the bullshit he put me through.

Deep down, I hated Adam for the way he dealt with our breakup. I felt he was irresponsible in the way he handled my heart. He made me feel as if my love wasn't worth it... as if I wasn't worth it. All the promises he made about our future were just empty words and that angered me. A huge part of me was resentful.

I was mainly angry at myself for opening up to someone that I thought loved me the same way I loved them. I felt fooled, betrayed, blinded by love or what I thought love was. And even though I knew he wasn't the person I expected him to be, I still gave him the benefit of the doubt that maybe someday he'd change and would apologize for being an asshole. But let's be honest, that's never happened.

I knew that in order to move on, and I mean fully move on, I needed to forgive him and forgive myself for putting my mind through so much torture.

Carrying around those feelings of resentment and anger disempowered me. I allowed these feelings, these thoughts, to occupy space in my head instead of letting them go. It's as if I didn't want my mind to be in peace.

Forgiveness is needed if you want to grow and want to evolve into a better version of yourself.

The first step is acknowledging that forgiveness doesn't mean you agree with what that person did to you. On the contrary, it's saying that you don't agree with what that person did to you but you're able to forgive them anyway. Their bad behavior shouldn't impact you forgiving them either.

It's important to note that forgiveness isn't a sign of weakness. It means you have the ability to let go of situations that are out of your control and you know that in order to move on with your life, you have to welcome happiness back into it. And you can only do that once you let go of the emotional baggage that's weighing you down.

I know it's hard to let go of your pain. I struggled with myself for years. I blamed myself and Adam for the situations and the pain I was going through. I felt my life was defined by my pain, when it really wasn't. Adding unnecessary stress to our hearts hurts our ability to focus and may also impact all the other relationships you have.

The longer you hold onto this pain, the longer it'll take you to get rid of it. Every day you choose to hold on to this pain is another day that goes by with you feeling like shit. That anger you have towards them isn't affecting them, it's affecting you. That should be a clear sign that you need to do something about it.

Stop letting people live rent-free in your mind. Start giving that open space to someone who deserves it and brings you peace of mind.

There's no point in beating yourself over this because if you can't forgive yourself, how are you going to live in peace in the future? How are you going to be happy again? Do you want to carry around this baggage for the rest of your life?

You have to decide you want better in order to get better, and that's exactly what I did.

You must forgive yourself first

To overcome guilt for things going wrong, you must forgive yourself.

You can't keep feeling guilty for letting people down. Shit happens. That's part of life. The only person you're really letting down is yourself by not being nicer to yourself. You deserve to relax, to breathe again, which means letting go of anything that's stressing you out.

Constantly blaming yourself for things that happened in the past isn't healthy. All you're doing is bringing back things that shouldn't be part of your present when you know it won't change the outcome. It won't change a thing so why waste more energy on it?

You might as well put that same energy on creating a better life for yourself. It's good to start over. You feel replenished and feel as though all the problems from the past are gone.

The only reason you feel forgiving yourself is difficult is because you're looking at it with 20/20 hindsight. Stop blaming yourself for things you cannot change. Learn from your mistakes instead of picking yourself to pieces.
I know what it feels like to feel guilty all the damn time and you're going to keep feeling that way until you master letting all that bullshit go.

Yes, you made mistakes in the past. Who hasn't? You're not the only one that's made silly decisions but to keep blaming yourself for them will only make you feel like crap. You have to accept that you did everything that you could to help your relationship grow and things didn't work out the way you expected them to… and that's okay. You can't change the past, but you can change the future.

Anytime you feel guilt coming on, remind yourself that you have the power to set yourself free. There are no locked doors. So, instead of letting guilt hold you like a prisoner, it's up to you to open the door and walk right out. You don't need to stay stuck in the past.

How is guilt going to benefit you in the long run? It won't. Guilt doesn't serve you in any way so the best thing to do is let it go.

One thing that helps many people is writing down what they feel guilty for. I've done this a few times and it's helped me realize that there were many things I couldn't have changed no matter how hard I tried and holding onto that guilt was only delaying me from moving forward.

I used to blame myself for not communicating with Adam as often as I should have. Maybe if I had said this or said that, things would be different. But would they really be different? Who knows but that wasn't a reason to stay stuck blaming myself.

Guilt will have you believing that maybe if you had done or said something, that things would have worked out, but the truth is, nobody knows what would've happened. And daydreaming about all those "what-ifs" isn't going to help you move on. If you stay stuck in this fantasy, false reality you're creating, you'll keep blaming yourself for things that already happened.

So, whenever you feel guilt sneaking up, write down things you did to try to make things work and show yourself compassion by realizing that you did all that you could.

Take responsibility for your part, acknowledge it and let it go. You see, you also have the responsibility to remove everything you're feeling and learning from it.

Forgive him

It's not easy. It'll take time but when you begin to shift your focus and stop dwelling on the pain they causes; you'll imagine yourself in a happier place. That's when you'll start making changes to your life.

Replace every negative thought you have about him with a positive one. In other words, you don't have to keep taking jabs at things he did to piss you off. You can easily shift your thoughts by believing that you're better off with someone else that's going to appreciate and value you. The more you do this, the less resentment you'll feel towards him.

Every time you have bad thoughts creeping in about things he put you through or made you feel, change your thoughts to something more positive. Once you do that, your feelings will change, and you'll slowly feel the urge to move on.

Many people have a hard time forgiving their ex because they want and expect closure. Let me keep it real with you. You don't need closure to move on with your life. It's not necessary to verbalize your forgiveness to the other person.
It only takes one person to forgive and that's you.

Forgiveness is truly about the dialogue you have with yourself, your heart and soul. You may never hear "I'm sorry" from your ex and it's okay because it's your choice to move on regardless. It'll be hard but you'll realize that your peace of mind is more important than having someone utter words they may not even mean.

Forgiving someone doesn't mean you have to forget what they did either. I've never believed in saying forgive and forget what the person did to you. That's pure bullshit. What you should be saying is forgive and grow from the experience you just went through.

Some people think that you have to be friends with your ex if you want to move on. This is sadly not true. Yes, it's important to keep a co-parenting relationship with them if you have kids together but that doesn't mean you have to necessarily be friends. The same applies to any other ex, just because you get along doesn't mean you have to force something that isn't there anymore.

Now don't get me wrong. There are many cases where staying friends with an ex helps people forgive them for the things they've gone through. But that's not always the case. Sometimes, not speaking to your ex anymore and letting go of that friendship helps you move forward. It's your decision to steer clear of him. No matter what you decide, avoid contact is it makes you feel uncomfortable.

Forgiving someone won't erase the hurt they caused during and after the breakup, but it will give you the opportunity to exhale and breathe again. It's your choice. It always starts with you.

Regardless of how long it takes you to move on, stand up and show them what you're truly made of. Just know that in the end, everything will be okay. You'll eventually have peace of mind and you'll feel like yourself again. Baby steps...

"Forgiveness and compassion towards
yourself will guide you towards
your healing process."

- M. Sosa

"I can still love you and never want to see you again. I have the right to protect my sanity especially if I feel being around someone hurts my heart."

- M. Sosa

"Just because he's giving you a little bit of attention doesn't mean he wants you back. Don't be a fool."

- M. Sosa

"Move on, beautiful.
You deserve better and you know it."

- M. Sosa

"My ex doesn't realize it, but he made me a better woman for someone else. Thank you for leaving when you did. It was a blessing in disguise."

- M. Sosa

"Someday, you'll meet someone that chooses you and only you. That'll be the day you realize why things didn't work out with someone else."

- M. Sosa

The brutal truth about breakups and relationships.

Other books by M. Sosa

- The Mistakes of a Woman – Vol 1
- Dilemma: The Quote Book
- The Mistakes of a Woman – Vol 2
- Letting Go: The Quote Book
- Things I Wish I Could've Told Him
- The Mistakes of a Man
- From Heartbreak to Self-love
- The Mistakes of a Woman – Deluxe Edition

All books can be purchased on Amazon, Barnes & Noble, BookDepository and other booksellers worldwide.

Instagram: @sweetzthoughts
Facebook: @sweetzthoughts

Moving On Isn't Easy
2019

Made in the USA
Coppell, TX
05 March 2020

16534997R00065